HAYDN

Symphony No. 103 in E-flat Major

The Score of the New Haydn Edition

Historical Background

Analysis · Views and Comments

NORTON CRITICAL SCORES

BACH   CANTATA NO. 4
edited by Gerhard Herz

BACH   CANTATA NO. 140
edited by Gerhard Herz

BEETHOVEN   SYMPHONY NO. 5 IN C MINOR
edited by Elliot Forbes

BERLIOZ   FANTASTIC SYMPHONY
edited by Edward T. Cone

CHOPIN   PRELUDES, OPUS 28
edited by Thomas Higgins

DEBUSSY   PRELUDE TO "THE AFTERNOON OF A FAUN"
edited by William W. Austin

HAYDN   SYMPHONY NO. 103 IN E-FLAT MAJOR ("DRUM ROLL")
edited by Karl Geiringer

MOZART   PIANO CONCERTO IN C MAJOR, K. 503
edited by Joseph Kerman

MOZART   SYMPHONY IN G MINOR, K. 550
edited by Nathan Broder

SCHUBERT   SYMPHONY IN B MINOR ("UNFINISHED")
edited by Martin Chusid

SCHUMANN   DICHTERLIEBE
edited by Arthur Komar

STRAVINSKY   PETRUSHKA
edited by Charles Hamm

Franz Joseph Haydn

SYMPHONY NO. 103
IN E-FLAT MAJOR

("*Drum Roll*")

The Score of the New Haydn Edition
Historical Background
Analysis · Views and Comments

Edited by

KARL GEIRINGER

PROFESSOR EMERITUS, UNIVERSITY OF CALIFORNIA, SANTA BARBARA

W · W · NORTON & COMPANY

New York · London

W. W. Norton & Company, Inc., 500 Fifth Avenue, New York, N.Y. 10110
W. W. Norton & Company Ltd., 37 Great Russell Street, London WC1B 3NU

Library of Congress Cataloging in Publication Data
Haydn, Joseph, 1732–1809.
  Symphony no. 103 in E-flat major (Drum roll)
  (Norton critical scores)
  Bibliography: p.
  1. Haydn, Joseph, 1732–1809. Symphony, M. 103,
E♭ major. I. Geiringer, Karl, 1899–   ed.
II. Series.
M1001.H4   785.1′154   73–20231

ISBN 0-393-09349-2

567890

Contents

Preface

To single out a particular symphony for the Norton Critical Scores from the extraordinary series that Haydn composed during his second London sojourn was not an enviable task. However, that No. 103, "with the Drum Roll"—which stands in the middle of the magnificent final trio, all of them completely written on English soil—deserves special attention will hardly be denied. Haydn here wrote a symphony that seems to embody the inventive power of a young genius rather than that of a man on the threshold of old age. At the same time, it is a work solidly based on experience gained during more than thirty-five years of symphonic composition—a garland selected from among the most inspired technical and formal devices he had used in earlier scores. Through the inclusion of highly subjective and experimental features, Haydn imbues these with a delightful character of their own.

Research on Haydn has not advanced as far as that on other great composers, notably Mozart. A collected edition of Haydn's works has not yet been completed, although the present (third) attempt seems likely to achieve fruition in the foreseeable future. Nor has any standard biography of the composer comparable to the Jahn-Abert for Mozart or Spitta for Bach yet appeared. Similarly, no large-scale studies exist that deal with individual symphonies in depth. H. C. Robbins Landon's excellent book *The Symphonies of Haydn,* the basic work on the subject, investigates the development of the form and aspects of its history, but offers no essays on specific compositions.

The present edition therefore includes shorter studies by several authors. None of these essays alone offers an exhaustive analysis, but they supplement each other; taken together they may provide a comprehensive picture. The student will even notice that in some instances the authors espouse differing viewpoints. In such cases it is up to the reader to weigh the evidence and take his own stand.

Tovey's brief essay, which the author himself designated as a "perfunctory analysis," is nevertheless written by a sensitive musician and provides insight into significant features of the symphony. The complementary analysis by the distinguished German musicologist Hermann Kretzschmar is preceded by a thoughtful discussion of Haydn's major contributions to the form of the symphony. H. C. Robbins Landon's comment on the Finale's monothematic structure supplements the sketchy treatment accorded this feature by the authors previously quoted. The quotations from Sir Henry Hadow and Rosemary Hughes deal with Haydn's use of Croatian folksongs. To wind up the analytical part of the essays, a paper by Marion Scott is presented, criticizing some of Tovey's statements and proceeding to a rather surprising explanation of Haydn's "secret." Her ideas must have seemed startling when they were first presented in 1942, but they do not necessarily appear so three decades later, since we have learned to observe similar features in the music of other 18th-century composers.

A final section offers comments of a more general nature, from the 18th and 20th centuries, about Haydn's symphonic achievement.

KARL GEIRINGER

HISTORICAL BACKGROUND

Unless specified otherwise, all numbered footnotes in the following essays are those of the respective authors.

Historical Background

The year 1790 witnessed a turning point in Haydn's career. For three decades he had presided over the vast musical establishment of the wealthy Hungarian princes of the Esterházy family. He composed and directed chamber music, orchestral music, operas, and church music, living alternately in the provincial city of Eisenstadt, in the Hungarian castle of Esterháza, and the Austrian capital of Vienna. In 1790 all this came to an end when Prince Nicholas ("the Magnificent"), a great patron of the arts and an admirer of Haydn's music, passed away. His successor was unwilling to continue spending vast sums for musical entertainment, and dismissed most of the musicians. While the composer kept his salary and his title as Prince Esterházy's Kapellmeister (director of music), he was a free man and master of his own fate.

It did not take long for new offers to reach him: Prince Grassalkovics, son-in-law of Haydn's deceased patron, wanted the composer to take charge of his band of musicians; King Ferdinand IV of Naples invited Haydn to come to his court; and the violinist and impresario J. P. Salomon offered excellent terms for work in London. Haydn's decision was easily made. He felt that at the court of the Prince or of the King he would again be a kind of high-class servant, while the stay in England offered the promise of respect and admiration from a music-loving community. Moreover, in Naples the emphasis would be on operatic music, while London with its excellent orchestras favored symphonic composition. Haydn no longer felt a strong interest in works for the stage—he must have realized that he could not compete with Mozart in this field—while instrumental music was his particular language. Thus he accepted Salomon's invitation (it is interesting that this decision to turn from aristocratic patrons to a bourgeois audience took place approximately at the time of the French Revolution).

3

On New Year's Day 1791 Haydn arrived in England, to stay there for a year and a half. During this period he shouldered a workload that might have crushed a younger man; yet the composer, who was nearing his sixtieth birthday, seemed to thrive on it. Between March 11 and mid-June 1791 he appeared in each of the twelve regular "Salomon Concerts" as well as in various benefit concerts; this schedule was repeated during the 1792 season. Invariably the first item on the second half of each program was a Haydn symphony, directed by the composer. Adding to this pressure was the artistic competition with his former pupil, Ignaz Pleyel—a contest that appealed to the sport-loving English, but which was easily won by the apparently nerveless Haydn. In July 1791 the composer traveled to Oxford to have the honorary degree of Doctor of Music conferred upon him and to attend three concerts in which compositions of his own, including the "Oxford" Symphony (No. 92), were performed.

Inspired by these great successes, and by the high regard shown to him by the English public, Haydn's creativity developed in the most prodigious manner. During the eighteen months in England the composer produced—apart from various smaller compositions—the opera *L'Anima del filosofo* (based on the Orpheus myth) and the first six of the "London," or "Salomon," symphonies (Nos. 93–98), works that surpass the best he had previously written in this genre.

At the end of June 1792, Haydn returned to Vienna. He worked there with his new pupil Beethoven and bought a house in a quiet suburb, but the idea of traveling to England for a second visit seems never to have left his mind. He wrote one symphony (No. 99) and started two others (Nos. 100 and 101) with a view to future performance in London, and before long his new negotiations with Salomon were concluded. Again, as on the first trip, he undertook to provide six new symphonies for concerts in the English capital.

Thus, early in 1794, at the age of sixty-two, Haydn started on the second great tour of his career, arriving in London on February 4. This time conditions were somewhat less hectic. He had emerged victorious from the rivalry with Pleyel and no new challenge to his abilities was planned. The impact of his concerts was perhaps less sensational, but they were no less enjoyed and cherished by the English public. During the first months of 1794 he participated also in various benefit performances. The following season, he worked no longer for Salomon, who, because of unsettled political conditions consequent upon the war with France, had been forced to discontinue his series. Haydn was engaged by the newly launched "Opera Concerts," under the artistic direction of the violinist G. B. Viotti. This put an unusually large and competent orchestra at his disposal, comprising sixty musicians: in all likelihood close to forty string players, two performers on each woodwind part, and one on each horn, trumpet, and timpani part. The climax of the season was reached at Haydn's benefit concert on May 4, 1795, when both the *Military* Symphony (No. 100) and Haydn's last symphony (No. 104) were performed. The composer remarked in his diary about this event:

> The hall was filled with a distinguished audience. . . . The whole society was extremely pleased and so was I. I netted four thousand florins on this evening. This one can make only in England.[1]

Before this, on March 2, at the second of the "Opera Concerts" at the King's Theatre, he had directed the first performance of Symphony No. 103 ("Drum Roll"). According to an entry in the autograph score, the work had been composed during 1795. The next day, in the *Morning Chronicle,* there appeared the following brief review:

> Another new Overture [a designation common at that time for symphonies] by the fertile and enchanting HAYDN, was performed; which as usual had continuous strokes of genius, both in air and harmony. The Introduction excited the deepest attention, the Allegro charmed, the Andante was encored[,] the Minuets, especially the Trio, were playful and sweet, and the last movement was equal, if not superior to the preceding.

The symphony was probably repeated at later concerts, possibly for the seventh "Opera Concert" on April 27 (the announcements and reviews of the day rarely refer to anything more specific than an "Overture"; the serial numbering of Haydn's symphonies now in use was made by Eusebius Mandyczewski for the incomplete edition of Haydn's works begun in 1908, and is now known to be not strictly accurate with respect to order of composition).

Haydn's final concert was on June 8, but he remained in England until August 15. His four seasons there had brought him a rich harvest of public acclaim and appreciation, as well as a small fortune that freed him from financial worry during his remaining years.

1. G. A. Griesinger, *Biographische Notizen über Joseph Haydn,* Leipzig, 1810, p. 53. Translation by the editor.

G. A. GRIESINGER †

Georg August Griesinger (d. 1828) was a minor official in the Saxon gov-
ernment whose major claim to fame was the intimacy of his relationship
with Joseph Haydn during the last ten years of the composer's life. His
work, *Biographische Notizen über Joseph Haydn,* was originally published in the *Allgemeine musikalische Zeitung* (Numbers 41–49, from July
to September 1809). His accounts of Haydn's life and times were sometimes at odds with historical fact, but the warmth and enthusiasm he
brought to his subject invested it with a unique quality. To quote Griesinger's own words: "My story may lay some claim to truth and accuracy,
and I hold it my duty often to intersperse Haydn's own words, just as I
wrote them down on returning home from him."

Vernon Gotwals, who translated and annotated the invaluable little
volume from which this excerpt is taken, is Professor of Music at Smith
College in Northampton, Massachusetts.

I asked him once in jest whether it was true that he had composed the
Andante with the Drum Stroke [Symphony No. 94] [1] to waken the English who fell asleep at his concert. "No," came the answer, "but I was
interested in surprising the public with something new, and in making a
brilliant debut, so that my student Pleyel, who was at that time engaged
by an orchestra in London (in 1792) and whose concerts had opened a
week before mine, should not outdo me. The first Allegro of my symphony had already met with countless Bravos, but the enthusiasm
reached its highest peak at the Andante with the Drum Stroke. Encore!
Encore! sounded in every throat, and Pleyel himself complimented me
on my idea." * * *

† From *Haydn: Two Contemporary Portraits.* A Translation with Introduction and
Notes by Vernon Gotwals of the *Biographische Notizen über Joseph Haydn* by
G. A. Griesinger and the *Biographische Nachrichten von Joseph Haydn* by A. C. Dies,
Madison, 1968, pp. 33–36. Reprinted by permission of the University of Wisconsin
Press.

1. Not to be confused with the subject of this volume, the Symphony No. 103,
"with the Drum Roll." [*Editor*]

Haydn had wished very much to hear something of his own work in the great London musicales arranged every year by the King, in which nothing but Handel's compositions was put on. He was given some hope of this, but a command soon appeared that at these musicales nothing composed less than thirty years ago might be performed. During his second stay in England, Haydn nevertheless succeeded. One of his symphonies was put on, and was excellently played by the royal orchestra. The King then wanted Haydn to conduct a Psalm by Handel from the organ. Haydn, who had studied Handel's works diligently, executed this mission to everybody's satisfaction.* * *

The King and the Queen wished to keep him in England. "You shall have a place in Windsor in the summers," said the Queen, "and then," she added with an arch look toward the King, "we shall sometimes make music tête à tête." "Oh!" replied the King, "I am not worked up over Haydn, he is a good honest German gentleman." "To keep that reputation," answered Haydn, "is my greatest pride." On repeated urging to remain in England, Haydn claimed that he was bound by gratitude to his Prince's house, and that he could not separate himself forever from his fatherland or from his wife. The King offered to send for the latter. "She will not cross the Danube, much less the sea," Haydn replied. He remained unmoved, and he believed that on that account the King never gave him anything. Of the royal family, only the Duchess of York came to his benefit concert, and she sent him fifty guineas. He was very kindly received by her several times, for she knew that her father, the King of Prussia, thought a great deal of Haydn. For the Prince of Wales he directed twenty-six musicales, and the orchestra often had to wait several hours before the Prince rose from the dinner table. Since this effort remained wholly unrewarded, Haydn at the advice of his friends sent from Germany a bill for a hundred guineas when Parliament settled the Prince's debts, and he was sent this sum without delay.

It was ill received and attributed to greed that Haydn presented his claim. As though Haydn should have spent for nothing on the heir to the English throne the time and effort he could so well economize! True delicacy will be less offended by the claim than by Haydn's having to claim what was his rightful due.

Dr. Burney first proposed to Haydn that he should be made a Doctor at Oxford. The ceremony of receiving the degree takes place in a cathedral with many solemnities. The doctors enter in procession and put to the candidates the question whether they wish to be admitted, and so forth. Haydn replied what his friend Salomon prompted. The election is put before the company from a platform. The speaker enlarged upon Haydn's merit, he cited his works, and at the question: Is Haydn admitted? there went up a general cry of assent. The doctors dress in a ruffle and a little mantle, and turn out in this costume for three days. "I really wished that my Vienna acquaintances had seen me in this outfit!" La Storace [2] and several other musical friends waved to him from the orchestra. The day after the election Haydn directed the music. As soon as he appeared, everyone called: Bravo Haydn! "I thank you!" he answered [in English], raising up the ends of the little mantle. This caused a great jubilee. Handel had spent thirty years in England without being accorded the honor of becoming a Doctor of Oxford.[3] It several times happened to Haydn that Englishmen walked up to him, surveyed him from head to foot, and left him saying [in English], "You are a great man."

Haydn received in London an ivory disk on a little blue ribbon with *Professional-Concert 1791* on one side, and with *Mr. Haydn* on the other; by showing this he was allowed free entry into the principal theaters, a courtesy never shown him in Vienna.

He earned in a three-year stay in England something like twenty-four thousand gulden, of which about nine thousand went for the journey, his support, and other expenses. He gave several persons lessons on the clavier, and each lesson was paid for with a guinea. "I opened my eyes wide at that!" * * *

Through long practice he had learned in general how musicians must be handled and thus succeeded by much modesty, by appropriate praise and careful indulgence of artistic pride so to win over Gallini's orchestra that his compositions were always well performed.

Haydn oftentimes repeated that he had become famous in Germany only by way of England.

2. Nancy Storace (1766–1817), a celebrated English soprano of Italian descent, sang the role of Susanna in the first performance of Mozart's *Le Nozze di Figaro* (Vienna, 1786). [*Editor*]

3. Griesinger's information is incorrect. Handel spent nearly half a century in London and he refused the proferred doctor's degree. [*Editor*]

THE SCORE
of the SYMPHONY

Edited by
HUBERT UNVERRICHT

ACKNOWLEDGMENT

This edition of Haydn's Symphony in E-flat major (No. 103) is printed by permission of G. Henle Verlag, München-Duisburg, from *Joseph Haydn Werke, Herausgegeben vom Joseph Haydn-Institut, Köln, unter der Leitung von Georg Feder, Reihe I, Band 18, Londoner Sinfonien, 4. Folge,* 1963, edited by Hubert Unverricht.

INSTRUMENTATION

2 Flutes (*Flauti*)
2 Oboes (*Oboi*)
2 Clarinets (*Clarinetti*): in B♭
2 Bassoons (*Fagotti*)
2 Horns (*Corni*): in E♭
2 Trumpets (*Clarini*): in E♭
Timpani in E♭, B♭

Violin I
Violin II
Viola
Violoncello
Double Bass (*Bassi*)

SYMPHONY NO.103 IN E-FLAT MAJOR

I: Adagio

I: Allegro con spirito

II: Andante più tosto Allegretto

II: Andante più tosto Allegretto

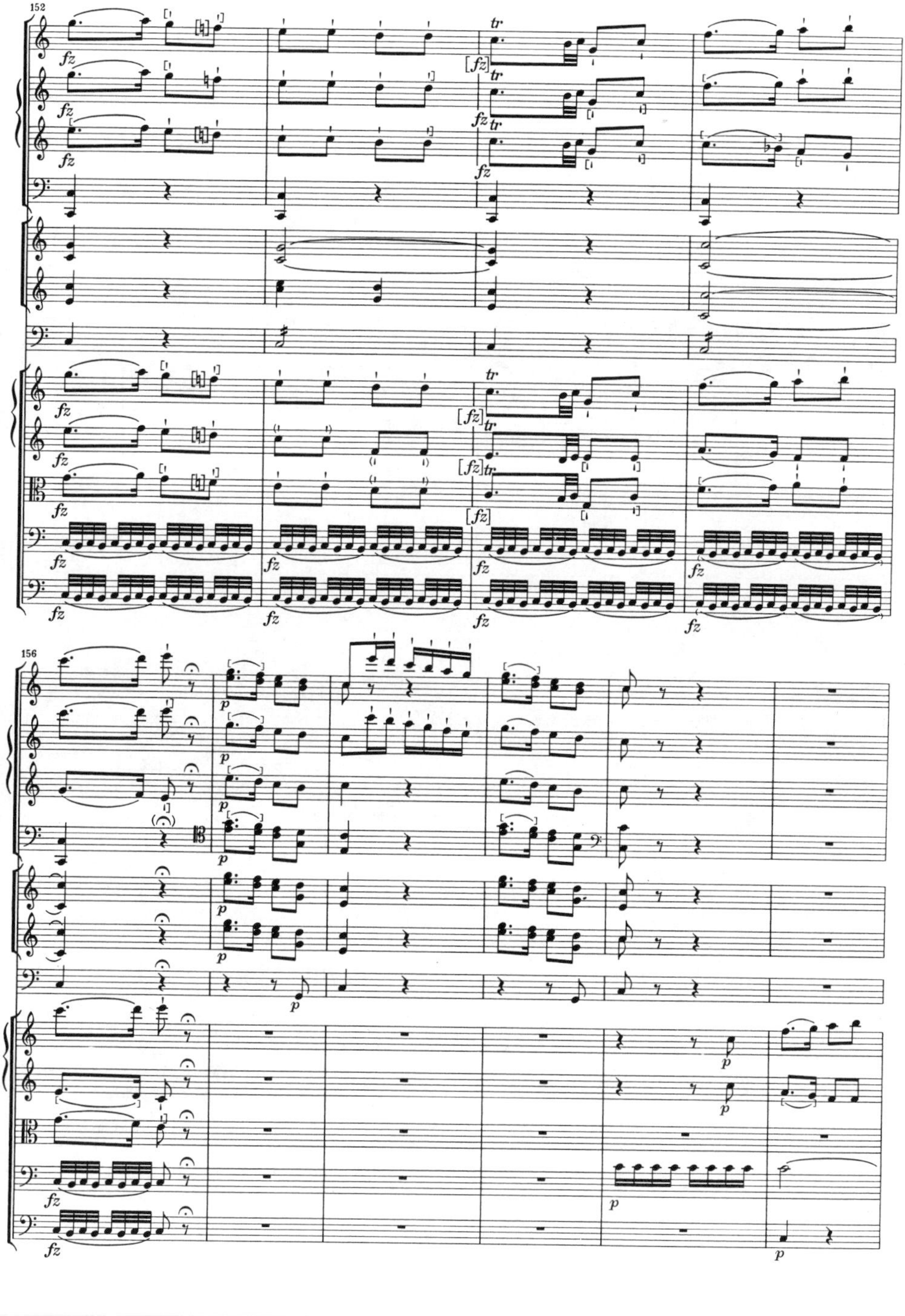
152
fz
tr
156
p

II: Andante più tosto Allegretto

Menuet

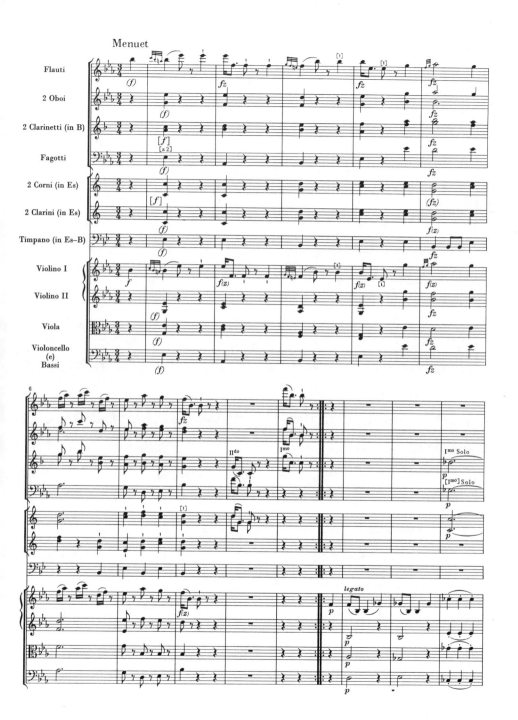

III: Menuet

III: Menuet

Trio

Menuet da Capo

IV: Finale: Allegro con spirito

IV: Finale: Allegro con spirito

IV: Finale: Allegro con spirito

IV: Finale: Allegro con spirito

*) The original ending follows on p. 83 ff.

Textual Note

The edition of the score here presented was prepared in 1962 by Dr. Hubert Unverricht for the new collected scholarly edition of Haydn's works published by G. Henle Verlag. The main sources used by Dr. Unverricht were Haydn's original autograph score (now in the British Museum, London) and the orchestral parts written by his amanuensis, Johann Elssler, which include numerous corrections and additions by Haydn (now in the Budapest National Library). The composer may have produced the score in January and February 1795, and he kept this autograph for more than a decade. In June 1805 Luigi Cherubini came from Paris to Vienna and brought Haydn a diploma and medal from the Paris Conservatory certifying his election to honorary membership in that venerable institution. The two musicians became close friends, and on the day preceding the premiere of Cherubini's opera *Faniska* Haydn presented him with the autograph score of Symphony No. 103. Under the original inscription, "di me giuseppe Haydn mp 795 Londra" ("by me, Joseph Haydn, and in my own hand, 1795, London"), the composer wrote "Padre del celebre Cherubini ai 24^{tro} di Febr. 806" ("father of the famous Cherubini, the 24th of February 1806"). Luigi Cherubini's grandson sold the score in July 1879 to Julian Marshall, from whom the British Museum purchased it soon afterward.

The autograph score is not quite complete. The first and the last pages of the third movement (mm. 1–21 of the Minuet and mm. 16–24 of the Trio) are written by an unknown hand, although the paper has the same watermark as the rest of the autograph. To the tempo marking "Andante" of the second movement the composer later added "più tosto Allegretto" and the signature "Haydn." On the empty last page of the score, two changes of the Finale's ending were inserted by Salomon. Measures 338–41 of the autograph were replaced by four new measures; similarly, for mm. 364–80, containing a surprising excursion to C♭, four new measures were substituted. This simpler and shorter version was certainly considered as definitive, as it is found in every other source; it is accord-ingly also used in our score. The original ending of the autograph is reproduced following this Textual Note.

Although Haydn occasionally inserted "Solo" or "Soli" into his wind parts, it is not always quite clear when the composer wanted the wind parts doubled and when he preferred to have them played by a single performer. Keeping the testimony of the sources in mind, Dr. Unverricht has attempted to present, with the help of brackets, a useful solution of this problem. The designation "Flauti" in the first movement of No. 103 is to be found in the autograph score and in the original performing part. Nevertheless, it does not seem quite certain whether one or two flutes are to play in this movement, or even whether changes between "Solo" and "a due" are intended.

EDITORIAL POLICY

In the present edition the musical text follows, as far as possible, the authentic sources while providing essential emendations and additions. Added dynamic signs, accidentals, slurs, etc., are placed in parentheses ( ), provided they are based on the testimony of secondary sources; they are placed in square brackets [ ] if they were inserted by the editor for obvious musical reasons, or on the basis of parallel passages. In the original ending of the Finale the signs $<$ $>$ are used for passages not completely written down in the original score but implied by such indications as "col basso."

Certain peculiarities of the original notation have been regularized:

1. The order of the instruments within the score and routine procedures of notation (writing out of abbreviations, direction of the stems, etc.) follow present-day usage.

2. If, in the autograph, two wind instruments are notated on the same line but with separate stems, they are in this edition usually notated with a single stem only.

3. Similarly, separate stems in the string parts are dispensed with if it is unlikely that *divisi* was intended.

4. Triplets are simply designated with the number 3.

5. The names of instruments and the expression marks (e.g., *cresc., staccato,* etc.) are spelled uniformly.

6. Accidentals unnecessary according to modern practice are omitted.

Apart from these specific instances, the present edition closely follows the authentic sources in notation. This is, in particular, true of the length of appoggiaturas, the notation of staccato signs (mostly lines, occasionally dots),[1] and, with few exceptions, the use of beams.

---

1. Haydn rarely used staccato dots. He employed them mainly in *piano* passages, when three or more notes of the same pitch were connected by a slur (e.g., first movement, mm. 113 and 115). His more standard symbols were short staccato lines above the notes.

THE ORIGINAL CONCLUSION
OF THE FINALE

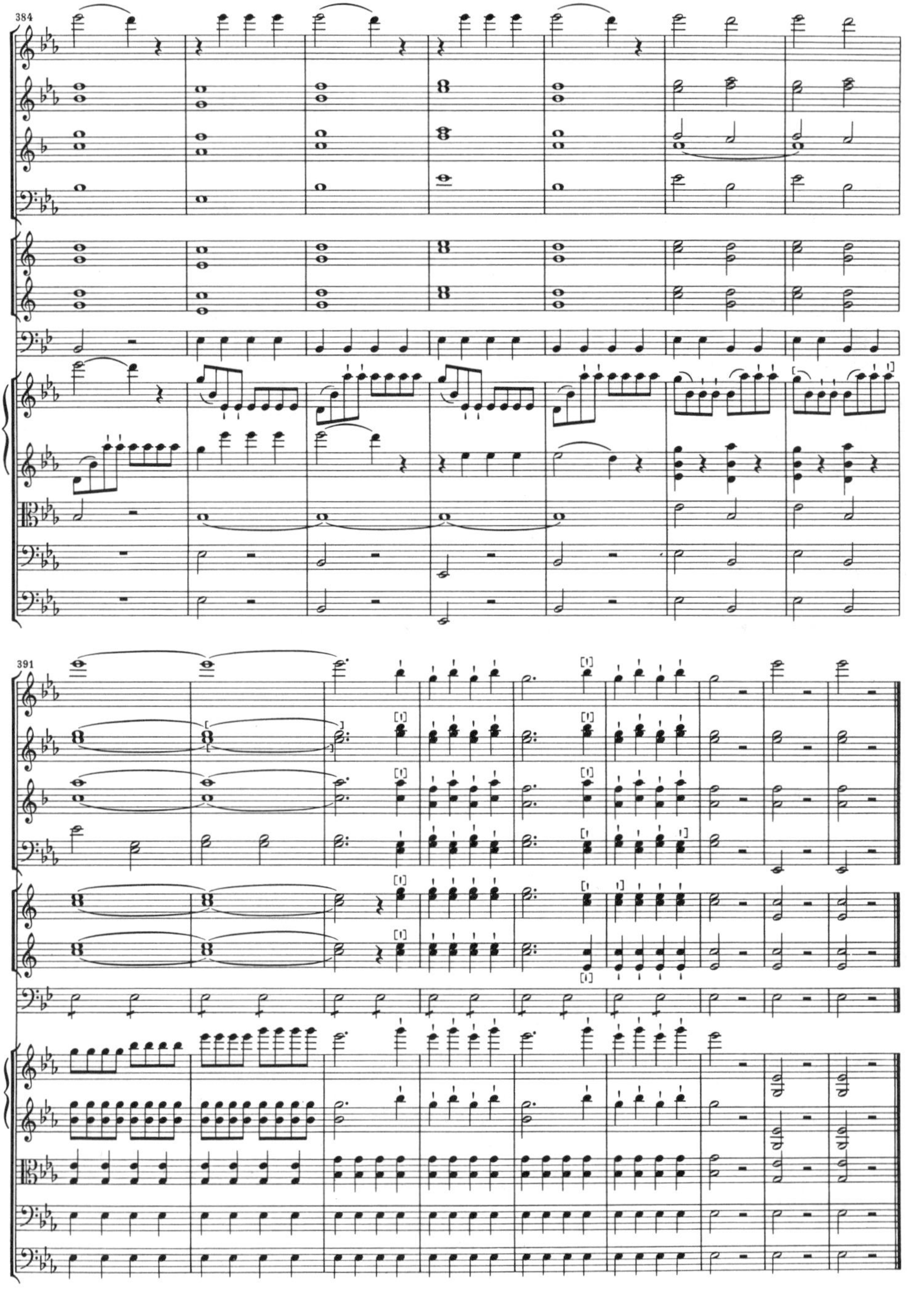
384
391

ANALYSIS

DONALD FRANCIS TOVEY†

Sir Donald Francis Tovey (1875–1940) was active as pianist, conductor, composer, and teacher. His reputation rests, however, primarily on his critical writings, most notably the six volumes of *Essays in Musical Analysis,* from which the present study of Haydn's Symphony No. 103 is taken.

Tovey was an excellent musician and a brilliant writer, who analyzed music from the point of view of the listener, not that of the scholar. He did not indulge in theoretical speculations but concentrated on features that would help the listener gain an appreciation of the works he heard performed. An enormously stimulating author, he often indulged in digressions, and at times even small factual errors crept in, as the reader of the present essay will observe. However, Tovey's infectious enthusiasm, his sense of humor, and, most of all, his deep insight into the essence of the work of art, make up for these minor shortcomings.

In the autograph this symphony is entitled "Londoner Symphonie No. 8". No task could be more futile than the attempt to range Haydn's twelve London Symphonies in order of merit. Their differences grow upon us with their merits as we emancipate ourselves from the doctrine which regards them as pianoforte duets with smashed-china climaxes tempered by the inhibitions of two nice little school-girls with flaxen pigtails.[1] As

† From *Essays in Musical Analysis,* London, New York, Toronto, 1948, I, 170–73. Reprinted by permission of Oxford University Press. Some of Tovey's music examples have been replaced by references, within brackets, to the score.
1. Tovey was writing in the days before modern long-playing recordings had replaced the piano as the primary home musical medium. Piano-duet arrangements of symphonic works were once very common (and, despite Tovey's reservations, they remain an admirable means for learning these works from the inside, as it were). [*Editor*]

I have remarked in analysing other symphonies of Haydn, the orchestration of these works, though deeply scarred with evidences of primitive conditions in orchestral performance, is equally wonderful for its power and its subtlety. Haydn's contemporaries found him noisy; and to-day our more sensitive disciples of Rimsky-Korsakov blame Beethoven for a treatment of the trumpets which is demonstrably less violent than Haydn's. We also ascribe to Beethoven's deafness the fact that his scores are full of interesting detail which seldom, if ever, reaches the listener's ear. But in any mature symphony of Haydn you will find that more detail is thus lost than in Beethoven's Ninth Symphony. And Haydn's detail is often lost beyond the recovering power of double wind and enthusiastic rehearsal; whereas to my knowledge accident or design has at one time and another brought to my ears every detail that my eye has ever read in Beethoven's scores. . . .

* * * Neither Haydn nor Beethoven ever thought that aesthetic economy implies that everything in a symphony directly reaches the ear. Their view was in part that of the Greek sculptors, who, arguing that the gods see everywhere, finished the backs of statues which were placed where no mortal eye would see more than the front. But there was also a more human view. Mr. Crummles's [2] leading tragedian could not put himself into Othello's skin until he had blacked himself all over. And the total experience of the players in a symphony is as that of the gods, who see everywhere. They play better all the time when their parts are more interesting than the listener realizes.

Although it is futile to compare the merits of Haydn's London Symphonies, it is permissible to compare their features. In this way we may venture to say that the Symphony with the Drum-roll is one of the most original of the twelve. Its forms are those most peculiar to Haydn and most unlike Mozart; and the opening drum-roll is merely the most obvious and the least remarkable of its unique features. The contemporaries of Beethoven must have forgotten the darkness of Haydn's introductory theme [mm. 1–7] if they thought Beethoven's genius more eccentric than that shown in this opening. Perhaps, however, they had become accustomed to make too much allowance for Haydn's notorious humour when such awe-inspiring tones came to their ears. And indeed it is true that when this introduction has come to its deepest gloom cheerfulness arises out of its last notes, just as it always broke in upon

2. Vincent Crummles was the eccentric but good-hearted manager of the Portsmouth Theater in Charles Dickens's *Nicholas Nickleby*. [*Editor*]

the philosophy of Dr. Johnson's friend Edwards [mm. 35–41].[3] Butter does not remain long unmelted in the mouths of Haydn's kittenish themes; and the full orchestra immediately bursts in with a new idea [m. 47]. But Haydn is in no hurry to change his key as yet; nor, when he changes it, does he at once introduce contrasted material. At last, however, a waltz strikes up [mm. 79–83] and is followed [4] by the solemn theme of the introduction transformed to something livelier than anything Mr. Edwards ever imagined [mm. 73–74]. The exposition as a whole is terse; but the development is unusually rich even for Haydn, who is always ready to expand. A new version of Ex. 1 [i.e., the theme from mm. 1–7] intervenes dramatically, in quick time but with something like the gloomy colour of the opening, and with chromatic wailings above it. The key is the tonic, but we do not realize that we are at home, and cheerfulness is more present to us when Ex. 3 [i.e., the theme from mm. 79–83] intervenes in the quite irrelevant key of D flat. After these and other adventures the tonic is again established on really convincing terms, and a more or less regular recapitulation follows. By way of coda the introduction reappears in its original tempo and is dismissed with laughter.

The andante is a set of variations in Haydn's favourite form, with two alternating themes, one in C minor and the other in C major. The minor theme is bleak in its two-part harmony, but full of ironic wit. Note the three turns of meaning given to the figure marked (*a*).

The second theme, allied in melody to the first, bursts out in full sunshine [mm. 27–30]. Haydn usually finds room for two full-sized variations of the first theme and one of the second; but here, as in the wonderful pianoforte Andante in F minor, he has room for two of the second, together with a very spacious coda. And so this movement ends happily in the major.

The Scotch snap which is prominent in the theme of the minuet [e.g., in mm. 2 and 4] indicates that into the courtly splendour of the famous minuet of Mozart's E flat Symphony an element has been introduced with which the Hof-Marschall has not been accustomed to deal.

---

3. Cf. the observations of Marion Scott, p. 30 below. [*Editor*]

4. Tovey has the order of these two examples reversed, as Miss Scott notes (*loc. cit.*). [*Editor*]

It is dealt with by the Great Bassoon Joke, aided by the horns. But this gives rise to graver thoughts; and the modulation, in the second part, to C flat and G flat is no joke. In the graceful trio, Haydn and Mozart meet on the common ground of a raillery in which the rustic is at no disadvantage with his urbane friend.

The finale begins romantically with the characteristic two-part harmony of horns and a phrase which is destined to blaze gloriously in the trumpets before the symphony is over. At present it serves as accompaniment to a melody that has been found, like many other of Haydn's themes, to be a Croatian folk-song:

* * *

Whether this theme has the honour to be Croatian or merely to be Haydn's own, it pretends to be a brand-new second subject when it appears later on in B flat with its phrase-accents turned round:

of this one. The end is inspired by the enthusiasm with which the trumpets take up the opening horn theme.

HERMANN KRETZSCHMAR †

~~~~~~~~~~

Hermann Kretzschmar (1848–1924), Professor of Music at the University of Leipzig and later Berlin, was one of the leading scholars of modern musicology emerging at the turn of the century. His *Führer durch den Konzertsaal*, a kind of German counterpart to Tovey's *Essays*, which analyzes orchestral and vocal literature from its inception, originally appeared in 1886 in three mammoth volumes. Subsequent editions extended the coverage into the first quarter of the 20th century. We draw here upon the most recent edition, the seventh, which was revised after the author's death by his pupil Friedrich Noack (1890–1958). Translated for the present volume are excerpts from the study on Haydn's symphonies in general and No. 103 in particular.

Haydn infused the spirit of the dance suite into the form of the Italian *sinfonia*. For those unaware of this transformation he added, as a special bonus, the minuet, the modernized *ländler*-like Austrian dance. The Allegro finale of the Italian *sinfonia* likewise conveyed the unaffected gaiety of a dance. In the other movements, however, fundamental differences prevailed between Haydn's idiom and the character of the Italian *sinfonia*. The first movement of the latter has broadly contoured, formal themes which, despite their triviality, strut on theatrical feet. Haydn, on the other hand, used—at least as a mature composer—concise, simple, natural, cheery, or warmly contemplative tunes which sound like folksongs but are of such innate nobility that they captivate and gladden even the most high-minded spirits.

His slow movements, the Adagios, Andantes, and Larghettos, display the profundity of J. S. Bach as well as the powerful emotionalism of Handel. They are alive with excitement; yet they mostly start from the realm of children's songs. Who wouldn't think in this connection of the Andante in the "Surprise" Symphony? These very movements lead back

† From *Führer durch den Konzertsaal, I. Abteilung,* "Sinfonie und Suite," 7th edition, revised and supplemented by Friedrich Noack, Leipzig, 1932, p. 115 ff. Reprinted by permission of Breitkopf & Härtel, Wiesbaden. Translated by the editor. Music examples have been replaced by references, within brackets, to the score.

to the parental cottage in Rohrau, to the evening hours when the father played the harp and the children sang to it. The family heritage and the atmosphere of Haydn's native country had a strong impact on his symphonies. They were partly responsible for his leaning toward the suite and for the wide circulation and enormous success his orchestral compositions enjoyed.

The popular character of Haydn's symphonies constitutes but one part of his innovation. Even more important than the invention of the musical ideas was their interpretation and development, the procedure which theologians and philosophers describe as the *exegesis*. In older instrumental music, fugue and variation were used to develop thematic content. Both techniques worked almost exclusively with the whole theme. On the other hand, there existed instrumental compositions, like the concerto, which employed fragments of the themes, so-called motives. Haydn made motivic development a guiding principle in the structure of his symphonies and chamber music, and he liked to work with motives that seemed of lesser significance within the context of the thematic material itself.

This novel procedure left intact the basic form of the Italian *sinfonia* in its first and last movements. In Haydn's first movements we find the traditional three main sections: exposition of the themes, their development, and recapitulation; thus, the structure of the so-called sonata movement. His finales either maintain the customary rondo form or use the sonata structure again. However, the individual sections are considerably enlarged by comparison to their counterpart in the *sinfonia*. This applies in particular to the development in the first movement, which constitutes its most important, exciting, and extensive section. If we view the presentation of musical ideas as the exposition in a drama, the development would appear as its most gripping scene, the catastrophe.

The slow movement was given a novel shape by Haydn. Either it follows in a general way the sonata structure of the first movement, though with a shorter development, or it takes the form of theme and variations. The variation form owes to Haydn's mastery its important position in the modern symphony, the string quartet, and other genres of instrumental music. In the period between the old orchestral suites of Haussmann and his followers and the creation of Haydn's works, variation form had led a modest existence, being used for clavier pieces and as an educational device.

The minuet alone maintains throughout the folk-music character that the other movements in Haydn's symphonies reveal only at the beginning when the themes are presented. The minuet consists of a main section divided into two parts, a contrasting trio, and a repeat of the main section. Both in form and content it never quite loses sight of its designation as a dance, and therefore it foregoes development, motivic elaboration, and all the artistry of the exegesis.

A surprisingly large number of music lovers feel for "Papa Haydn," the "childish" Haydn, an admiration tinged with a touch of condescension, because the themes of his famous symphonies make him appear as an easygoing good fellow moving within a circle of rather superficial ideas. These critics entirely overlook the relationship between Haydn's themes and the works of the Berlin song school. In particular, they pay no attention to the method whereby the themes are elaborated. Haydn's manner of developing his ideas, exploiting them, and building them up to extensive compositions does not presuppose significant musical ideas; only rarely can such themes be used for his purpose. Likewise the gift of first invention, the free flow of thematic inspiration is of little value for his technique. Themes suited for Haydn's method must be clear-cut, divisible, and, most of all, endowed with an unlimited capacity for transformation. The essence of Haydn's symphonies is not to be found in the themes themselves, but in the composer's artful treatment of them. Haydn was motivated by the same belief that made Aeschylus and Sophocles base their tragedies on folk legends, that let Schütz and Handel employ for their compositions commonplace subjects or inventions by others: they all believed that the originality and substance of the basic ideas was less important to the finished product than the artist's mastery of his materials. A symphonic composer wishing to achieve results with Haydn's method has to be endowed with an extremely rich and flexible mind; he must be able to illuminate a single theme with a thousand different kinds of lighting and to allow it to open up all the gates to his emotional and imaginative life. He must be joyfully aware of the wealth and unique nature of his own personality and feel free to communicate of his inner self whatever seems fitting. While the *sinfonia* before Haydn was a festive music, it became through him a composition of a most intimate nature. The composer's subjectivity was allotted a much wider scope than orchestral music had heretofore known. Since Haydn it has been, as Brahms remarked, "no longer a joke to write a symphony."

In addition to introducing the spirit of the suite and stressing motivic elaboration, Haydn carried out a third innovation. Starting with the compositions of his middle period, he eliminated the harpsichord from the orchestra. Like the incorporation of the minuet and his use of popular themes for the symphonies, this constitutes a rapprochement with contemporary folk music. As soon as the instruments in Haydn's orchestra parted with the harpsichord, they enjoyed a freedom of inter-course unknown in earlier compositions. Solo passages alternate between the different instruments with a flexibility that, though attempted pre-viously by Handel (in his oboe concertos), C. P. E. Bach, and the Mann-heim school, had never been achieved in the manner carried out by Haydn. As the privilege of appearing as soloist was now allotted to every instrument and was exercised in diverse ways, orchestral sound was greatly enriched through new coloristic effects which contributed largely to the symphonies' effects on Haydn's contemporaries. However, we today often have no conception of the beauty and singularity of Haydn's orchestration, since we spoil it through the lack of balance between strings and woodwinds, thus injuring particularly Haydn's art of mixing colors. Modern conductors should be familiar with the exact size of the orchestra customary in Haydn's time and plan their performances accord-ingly. Without some historical knowledge one cannot do justice to the so-called classic composers.

Among Haydn's innovations in the symphony, the principle of motivic elaboration is by far the most important. It has determined the future of this form up to our time. Its spirit and its nature were deeply rooted in Haydn's personality. With his acumen, his quick repartee, his wit, he was born to bring this method to fruition.

[Symphony No. 103] belongs among Haydn's numerous symphonies in the key of E-flat major. Like most of the composer's later symphonies, it begins with a meditative and romantic introduction preceding the first Allegro [mm. 1–7]. In such introductions are gathered the loftiest ideas conjured up by the composer when he envisioned the complete work. Conceived in accordance with the character of the particular symphony, they differ widely from each other, and especially from their original model, the first Largo of the French overture. . . . The present introduc-tion is particularly significant. Haydn quotes from it twice in the course of the following Allegro. The first time, its serious features appear in fast tempo and only for a fleeting moment, in the development after the first fermata (m. 111); when the recapitulation is finished the composer introduces it once more, and this time in its original version.[1] Such recurrences of the introduction in the course of the main movement are rare in Haydn's symphonies; the fact that this happens in No. 103 proves the significance of this specific introductory theme. The composer was fascinated by it and therefore did not fully surrender to the gay mood of the Allegro's two main themes [mm. 35 and 79].

The movement is far more inclined toward seriousness than one would anticipate from its light and merry principal subjects. As to its formal structure, this Allegro appears to be an ordinary sonata movement, of a regularity rarely to be found in Haydn's works. There is a sharply profiled second subject, and the key relationship between first and second subjects is the obligatory one: tonic–dominant. In his development sections Haydn often liked to tease the listener by introducing a mock recapitulation, which presents the main subject in the tonic key long·before the actual recapitulation takes place. In this symphony, however, despite the ingenuity and the wealth of invention displayed, he adheres to established rules.

Equally typical is the construction of the third section, the recapitulation. We find in it a simple though somewhat condensed restatement of the first section, with the traditional modifications of key. Only the coda pursues a path of his own. Here the theme of the introduction enters the merry assembly like a ghost. This is quite unusual and forces us to admire the liberties taken by genius. A peculiarity of Haydn's style, the predilection for sudden emphatic stops—an impressive and startling rhetorical device resulting from his study of French music—manifests itself with particular intensity in this movement. It contains no less than six eloquent fermatas! In the orchestration, the use of clarinets is worth noticing; Haydn became familiar with these instruments only during his stay in England.

The second movement, an Andante, starts with a theme full of dark beauty, which assumes a character of its own through the use of augmented seconds [mm. 1 ff.]. An extended tune in two-part song form grows out of this remarkable beginning. It is followed by a parallel section of marchlike character. By transforming the original C-minor melody into the major mode and applying slight rhythmic changes, Haydn manages to provide this parallel section with completely new features [mm. 27 ff.]. Two variations on both the main and the parallel themes

1. Cf .the statements on p. 19 and p. 32 of this volume. [*Editor*]

follow. The first variation of the major melody introduces a violin solo. Its ending, softly dying away, effectively contrasts with the powerful beginning of the second minor variation, which uses all the instruments, including brass and kettledrums. The movement testifies again to the fact that the art of writing variations entered a new phase with the advent of Haydn's symphonies. The composer's genius manifests itself especially in the coda beginning after the fermata (m. 157). This is a free postlude to the set of variations, a poetical farewell in which all the preceding ideas and moods are once more recapitulated and thereby intensified. The sixteen measures from the startling entrance of the dominant-seventh chord in A (m. 171) to the return of the major theme (m. 187) belong among the art's most inspired and original ideas. It has been rightly stated that this Andante, and in particular its coda, may well have served as a model for the funeral march of Beethoven's *Eroica*.

The third movement is a Minuet. The unusual melodic and rhythmic aspects of the first subject [mm. 1 ff.] show from the outset that this movement is more than a simple dance. Haydn presents here a significant character piece which, despite its formal simplicity and easy melodic flow, occasionally reveals profundity and pathos through the use of daring modulations. The Trio displays even greater freedom of invention; this is particularly true of the episode in which the violins gaily take up the utterances of the horns (m. 57).

The finale is based on the single subject [mm. 5 ff.]. It is amazing how many varying and beautifully cohesive episodes are derived from the few notes of this simple melody. Haydn develops it with a magnificent display of contrapuntal art. The spirit of Mozart seems to manifest itself in this composition, as in other movements from the London symphonies. The heartfelt friendship which the old master felt for the younger composer is thus proclaimed. Mozart's death seems only to have further deepened these sentiments.

H. C. ROBBINS LANDON †

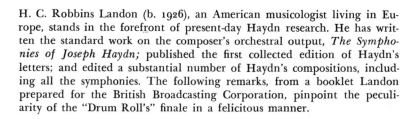

H. C. Robbins Landon (b. 1926), an American musicologist living in Europe, stands in the forefront of present-day Haydn research. He has written the standard work on the composer's orchestral output, *The Symphonies of Joseph Haydn;* published the first collected edition of Haydn's letters; and edited a substantial number of Haydn's compositions, including all the symphonies. The following remarks, from a booklet Landon prepared for the British Broadcasting Corporation, pinpoint the peculiarity of the "Drum Roll's" finale in a felicitous manner.

All his life Haydn experimented with monothematicism: that is, with the possibility of dropping the second subject altogether or, at any rate, rendering it structurally of secondary importance. In No. 103/IV he constructs the whole movement on one theme, and thereby sets himself a particularly hard task; needless to say he brings it off with dash and vigour, and it is an astonishing tribute to his ingenuity that although there is only one theme, it is varied so deftly that one is hardly conscious of the all-present monothematicism. By way of introducing the theme, he has a short fanfare for the horns, a series of chords which also prove to be the accompaniment of the principal subject. In essence, Haydn has now created a form where all the individual parts, however secondary they may at first appear, have a vital structural task to fulfil.

† From *Haydn Symphonies,* BBC Music Guides, Seattle, University of Washington Press, 1969, p. 63.

W. H. HADOW †

Sir William Henry Hadow (1859–1937), editor of the original *Oxford History of Music* and author of its fifth volume, *The Viennese Period,* also wrote monographs on English music, Beethoven, and Wagner. He enthusiastically supported the ideas of the Croatian musicologist Frantisek X. Kuhač, who claimed that Haydn was of Croatian origin.[1] Although this theory has been totally discredited by modern research,[2] the startling statements of both Kuhač and Hadow concerning the origin of some basic themes in Haydn's Symphony No. 103 are still considered valid in some quarters.[3]

Haydn's music is saturated with Croatian melody; the resemblances are beyond attribution of coincidence, beyond any explanation but that of natural growth. Some of his tunes are folksongs in their simplest form, some are folksongs altered and improved, the vast majority are original, but display the same general characteristics.*** No doubt can exist as to the Symphony in E♭ "Mit dem Paukenwirbel." [4] ***The Andante is founded on two themes, the first minor—[mm. 1–8]—the second major—[mm. 27–50]—both of which are taken and considerably improved from two folksongs of the Oedenburg district, (a) *Na Travniku*

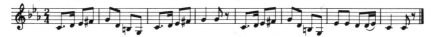

† From *A Croatian Composer. Notes Toward the Study of Joseph Haydn,* London, 1897, p. 37 ff. Some of the music examples have been replaced by references, within brackets, to the score.

1. Frantisek X. Kuhač, *Josip Haydn i Hrvatske Narodne Popievke,* Zagreb, 1880.

2. Cf. Ernst Fritz Schmid, *Joseph Haydn: ein Buch von Vorfahren und Heimat des Meisters,* Kassel, 1934, p. 12 ff.

3. Michel Brenet (*Haydn,* Paris, 1909, p. 153 f.) complained, however, that the Croatian folksongs presented by Kuhač in support of his theory were collected during the 19th century and that no documents antedating the time of Haydn can be found to prove the authenticity of these tunes.

4. German for "with the Drum Roll." [*Editor*]

and (b) *Jur Postaje,*

while the principal tune of the Finale—[mm. 5–12]—is that of the song *Divorjčica potok gazi*

which is common among the Croats, especially those of Haydn's district.

ROSEMARY HUGHES[†]

Rosemary Hughes, British musicologist, has written a sensitive book on Haydn, as well as a study on the composer's string quartets for the "BBC Music Guides." In the following passage she comments interestingly on Haydn's use of folksong in Symphony No. 103.

What is indeed remarkable is the racy twist with which [Haydn] not only lifts them out of the commonplace but also gives them the stamina to move symphonically. In the alternating variations that make up the Andante of the Drumroll Symphony (No. 103), the minor melody (a Croat tune from Sopron,[1] near Eisenstadt) is originally a symmetrical affair, subsiding on to its tonic; by the time Haydn has finished with it, it has become a sinewy, free-modulating creature, able to carry some of his finest scoring and contrapuntal ornament, while in the major tune (another folk melody) he has only to sharpen the F in the ascending scale (matching the minor tune) to give it that spark of originality which, in the coda, kindles into an incandescent blaze of poetry.

† From *Haydn*, London and New York, 1950, p. 115. Reprinted by permission of the publisher, J. M. Dent.
1. The Hungarian name for Oedenburg. [*Editor*]

MARION M. SCOTT†

Marion Scott (1877–1953), British violinist and music critic, wrote a number of valuable studies on Haydn and his music. Her paper *Haydn: Fresh Facts and Old Fancies* reveals her critical mind, and also her attempt to explore hitherto unplumbed depths in Haydn's work.

Miss Scott states that, according to Giuseppe Carpani, the author of one of the composer's earliest biographies, Haydn based his works on a secret formula whose nature he refused to divulge, and proposes an answer to this riddle.

Haydn's method was pre-eminently flexible, not lapidary, and definitions are therefore difficult. Here is one I have tried to make: "The *melodic dimensions* of the *first notes* of the *first subject* of the *first movement* are the source of the whole work." Or, to give a fuller definition—"The notes which initiate a work constitute a 'motto' or 'germ' theme, from whose first melodic intervals may be derived at will the main subjects, tonalities and harmonies, and even the proportions of the entire work."

Haydn designed this method for instrumental music. The first glimmerings of it came to him early in life and his earliest essays in it were tentative and incomplete. As his imagination and craftsmanship increased he gradually expanded and enriched it until, in his maturest works, it found its fullest expression.***

As an example of his "secret" in operation, take his Symphony in E♭, No. 103, known as "The Drumroll." It was almost his last symphony and composed in 1795.

It opens with a soft mysterious drumroll on E♭. Then a slow theme, which forms the introduction, begins to wind its way up the lower register of the cellos, basses and bassoons.

† From *Haydn: Fresh Facts and Old Fancies* in *Proceedings of the Musical Association,* Sixty-eighth Session, 1941–42, p. 92 ff. Reprinted by permission.

From this theme the elements Haydn appears to have elected to develop were the 1, 3 and 6, with the semitones as tributaries in their capacity of steps of one degree.

That *Introduction,* thirty-nine bars long, leads into the main *Allegro.* Note the insistence in the bass of the cadence pause (prefacing the *Allegro*) on the step of one degree, reiterated three times with a *sforzando* on each A♭ to make the semitone more emphatic. The *Allegro con spirito* opens with a theme which *seems* new. Dr. Kuhač and Sir Henry Hadow both stated this was a Croatian folksong. It may be, but its first notes are also the "clue" intervals of the *Introduction* turned slightly inside out—the step of the semitone going up and the interval of the third made conjunct by a filling-up note. Haydn however makes the 1 and 3 stand out as the prominent notes by the way in which he disposes emphasis. It may be chance or it may be intentional that the most arresting feature of the second subject is a sixth. But it is beyond dispute that it is prefaced by a passage which Sir Donald Tovey described as "the solemn theme of the introduction transformed to something livelier than anything Mr. Edwards ever imagined" (Mr. Edwards being of course that friend of Dr. Johnson's whose cheerfulness always broke through). By a curious slip Tovey says the transformed theme of the *Introduction* follows the second subject—but the score shows that it precedes it, a beautiful bit of Haydn's logic.

The development starts in B♭ major, the orthodox key, and deals first with the first subject of the *Allegro;* towards the end of that eighteen-bar section it cadences on to G major with emphasis. Note that the key of G major is a third below B♭ major, thus expressing the idea of the third in the "clue" or "germ" theme—and, incidentally, that G major stands a third above the original tonic of E♭. Next in the development Haydn treats the theme of the *Introduction* in diminution in the bass while the upper strings express the idea of the semitone, the steps of one degree in the "germ" theme, by constant little chromatic murmurings. The second subject, which is treated last in the development, appears in what Tovey calls "the quite irrelevant key of D♭." By academic rules it is irrelevant but in point of fact it is fairly relevant to the "germ" theme, for D♭ major is a key from which Haydn can drop a minor third—as he does—to the important cadence on to B♭ major, the dominant, which announces the recapitulation and return to the tonic key of E♭ major.

The recapitulation reproduces the exposition fairly regularly, except that the quick variant of the motto theme of the *Introduction* (which originally led to the second subject) is replaced by a passage in which the first violins simply shout out their clue of "one" degree. The recapitulation is followed by a remarkable coda beginning with the motto theme of the mysterious slow *Introduction* in its original tempo, which, after twelve bars, flashes back to *Allegro* for the sixteen bars ending the movement. Tovey said of this in his analysis: "By way of coda the *Introduction* reappears in its original tempo and is dismissed with laughter." He missed its significance; those sixteen quick bars at the end are the motto theme in their *Allegro* disguise. They prefaced the second subject in the exposition but did not do so in the recapitulation. Here, in the coda, is the explanation. Haydn uses them as the logical continuation of the recapitulation of the *Introduction* and then rounds off the whole movement with playful allusions to the first and second themes of the *Allegro*. It is all as satisfying to close reason as productive of sheer delight.

Space does not allow such close analysis of the other movements, but they are nearly as fascinating in their design and craftsmanship. The second movement (*Andante*) is a set of variations in C upon two themes, one of which is in the minor, the other in the major. Note that this key of C is the third below E♭ major, and is derived quite logically from the "clue" theme. Kuhač and Hadow give these themes as folksongs from the Oedenburg district. Very possibly they are, but Haydn's treatment of them all his own. He wished, I think, to present the interval of the third in both its aspects, major and minor, and the minor third even in the disguise of an augmented second. The upper note of that augmented second (the F♯ rising to G) fairly hammers into one's hearing the other "clue" interval—the step of one degree.* * *

The *Minuet* looks superficially as if it had nothing to do with the "clue," but it is permissible to wonder whether the turn which lies between its first and second notes and which is an integral part of the theme, is not a subtle exposition of the step of one degree in the clue theme.

In the *Trio* the theme is so contrived that whenever the interval of the third occurs, as it does ten times in eight bars, it specially claims notice. Is this accident or design? I will not say.***

The *Finale* is a big intricate movement, said to be founded on yet another Croatian folksong. This particular theme is not closely relevant to the "clue" theme unless it be regarded as a kind of expansion of the clue, rather as a rubber ring will pull out to twice its size. It may, or may not, express the step of one degree in the clue by its conjunct motion. But I have small doubt that the bars for horns alone, which open the movement with a phrase of "horn-fifths" and which cover in conjunct motion the intervals of the *rising and falling* third do contain an allusion to the "clue." This phrase is not a mere prefatory summons to attention; it seems as if it were the subject to which the folk theme—the ostensible first subject—is the countersubject. The horn-fifths subject appears at various points throughout the *Finale,* and at the climax, close to the end, it is blazed out by the horns and trumpets, a sure indication Haydn considered it important. The main return to the key of E♭ major for the recapitulation is made not from the dominant B♭ major as is customary, but direct from G major; the falling third again in fact! [1]

1. Miss Scott proceeds to speculate on the proportions of the movements, the significance of the number of bars in individual sections and movements, and on their "digits" (resulting from the sideways addition of the figures in a larger number), ruminations which seem to exceed the purpose of the present volume. [*Editor*]

VIEWS AND COMMENTS

CHARLES BURNEY †

~~~~~~~~~~

Charles Burney (1726–1814), British organist, composer, and musical his-torian, was a shrewd and penetrating observer of the musical scene in his own time. He traveled widely on the continent, establishing personal con-tacts with leading musicians and furnishing interesting and amusing re-ports about his experiences. Burney felt great admiration for the works of Haydn, and it was largely due to his efforts that the composer was awarded the honorary doctorate from Oxford University. As early as 1789, two years before Haydn's first visit to England, Burney wrote about him in his remarkable *A General History of Music.*

[Haydn] is now as much respected by professors for his science as inven-tion.[1] Indeed, his compositions are in general so new to the player and hearer, that they are equally unable, at first, to keep pace with his inspiration. But it may be laid down as an axiom in Music, that "what-ever is *easy* is *old,* and what the hand, eye, and ear are accustomed to; and, on the contrary, what is *new* is of course *difficult,* and not only scholars but professors have it to learn. The first exclamation of an embarrassed performer and a bewildered hearer is, that the Music is very *odd,* or very *comical;* but the queerness and comicality cease, when, by frequent repetition, the performer and hearer are at their ease. There is a general chearfulness [*sic*] and good humour in Haydn's allegros, which exhilerate [*sic*] every hearer. But his adagios are often so sublime in ideas and the harmony in which they are clad, that though played by inarticu-late instruments, they have a more pathetic effect on my feelings, than the finest opera air united with the most exquisite poetry. He has like-wise movements that are sportive, *folâtres,* and even grotesque, for the sake of variety; but they are only the *entre-mets,* or rather *intermezzi,* between the serious business of his other movements.

† From *A General History of Music from the Earliest Ages to the Present Period* (1789), newly edited by Frank Mercer, New York, 1957, II, 959 f.

1. The extent of Haydn's fame may be imagined from his being made the hero of a poem called *The Art of Music,* in Spanish, and printed in Madrid ten years ago.

ANONYMOUS (1794)†

The London correspondent of the Weimar *Journal des Luxus und der Moden* published, on March 25, 1794, an enthusiastic report on Haydn's string quartets that included the following comment about the reception of the London symphonies.

But what would you now say to his new symphonies, composed expressly for these concerts and directed by himself at the pianoforte? It is truly wonderful what sublime and august thoughts this master weaves into his works. Passages often occur that render it impossible to listen to them without becoming excited. We are altogether carried away by admiration and forced to applaud with hand and mouth. This is especially the case with Frenchmen, of whom we have so many here that all public places are filled with them.[1] You know that they have great sensibility and cannot restrain their transports, so that in the midst of the finest passages in soft adagios they clap their hands in loud applause and thus mar the effect. In every symphony of Haydn the adagio or andante is sure to be repeated each time after the most vehement urging. The worthy Haydn, whose personal acquaintance I highly value, behaves on these occasions in the most modest manner. He is indeed a goodhearted, candid, honest man, esteemed and beloved by all.

† Quoted in K. F. Pohl and Hugo Botstiber, *Joseph Haydn,* Leipzig, 1927, III, 76. Translation by the editor.
1. The French Revolution and its aftermath were, of course, responsible for this refugee population. [*Editor*]

PAUL HENRY LANG†

Paul Henry Lang (b. 1901), for many years Professor of Musicology at Columbia University, is noted as both scholar and critic (for the New York *Herald Tribune* [1954–63]) and indeed represents an unusually profound combination of the two sensibilities. His writings, particularly the monumental *Music in Western Civilization*—source of the present extract—are significant for their emphasis on music's position within the framework of general culture. Despite the breadth of his interests, he seems to have a predilection for the 18th century.

In the symphonies written for London, Haydn reached the ideal balance of homophony and a specific modern instrumental polyphony, thematic and melodic rather than rhythmic and motivic. This gave him a freedom of imagination heretofore unknown. What a fantastic cavorting of melodies, rhythms, syncopations, dynamic contrasts, general pauses, hesitations, sudden explosions, distortions, their maze skillfully manipulated by the subtle employment of the high art of double counterpoint carried into the smallest particular. Detail in composition—and the real artist shows in details especially the most thorough craftsmanship—is derived from the whole and leads back to it. What makes Shakespeare's characters great is that the poet develops, above all, those traits in their nature and mentality from which their destiny, their rise or fall, originates. It is in this way that dramatic actions achieve their sense of unity. Haydn proceeds in the same manner, but his characters and figures are abstract. In his development of the thematic element he gives the essential by eliminating everything that is secondary or that has no bearing on the destiny of his subjects. The detail serves him in working out the character of his motives, in leading them into a situation which enables them to present the solutions of their destinies as inevitable natural phenomena.

† From *Music in Western Civilization*, New York, 1941, p. 631 f.

KARL GEIRINGER †

The mosaic style of the thematic development has become a matter of course; filling and accompanying voices enjoy the same privileges as the parts carrying the melody, for the same motives are used by all. The baroque division into leading instruments, whose parts are florid and ornamental, and subordinate instruments, whose function is that of giving a foundation to the evolutions of the others, reflects the social cleavage of the period into a ruling and a subservient class, a division that here has been abandoned entirely.

*   *   *

The most remarkable feature of these compositions written in the nineties is that they occasionally present a somewhat problematical and experimental character. They show a definite tendency toward trying out new devices, even at the sacrifice of the poise of former years. Fundamentally, Haydn remained a classical composer, but again and again episodes are to be found in his music in which expressiveness and passionate feeling break through classical composure. Under the influence of the new experience of freedom, Haydn's musical style lost some of its former restraint. He seemed to revive characteristic features of his storm-and-stress period. But we shall be nearer the truth if we consider the little irregularities in his later music to be the first indications of a movement that was shortly to exercise a profound influence over the whole artistic world: romanticism.

† From *Haydn, a Creative Life in Music,* 2nd ed., revised and enlarged, Berkeley and Los Angeles, 1968, pp. 353 and 338. Reprinted by permission fo the University of California Press.

CHARLES ROSEN[†]

Charles Rosen (b. 1927) is an unusually versatile American scholar and artist, who earned a doctorate in French literature at Princeton University while appearing successfully as a concert pianist. His searching and perceptive work *The Classical Style: Haydn, Mozart, Beethoven* won the 1972 National Book Award in the category of Arts and Letters. At present he serves on the faculty of the State University of New York in Stony Brook.

The symphonies of Haydn are heroic pastoral, and they are the greatest examples of their kind. I am alluding not only to the deliberately "rustic" sections of the symphonies—the bagpipe effects, the Ländler rhythms in the trios of the minuets, the imitation of peasant tunes and dances, the melodies based on yodeling. Even more characteristic is the pastoral tone, that combination of sophisticated irony and innocence that is so much a part of the pastoral genre. The rustics in pastoral speak words whose profundity is apparently beyond their grasp; the shepherds are not aware that their joys and sorrows are those of all men. It is easy to call the simplicity of the pastoral artificial, but it is this simplicity which is most moving, the country simplicity that speaks with a sharp nostalgia to the urban reader. The symphonies of Haydn have that artful simplicity, and, like the pastoral, their direct reference to rustic nature is accompanied by an art learned almost to the point of pedantry. Haydn's most "rustic" finales generally contain his greatest display of counterpoint. Nevertheless, the apparent naïveté is at the heart of Haydn's manner.

† From *The Classical Style*, New York, 1971, p. 162. Reprinted by permission of The Viking Press, Inc.

Bibliography

THE MUSIC

Joseph Haydn, Kritische Ausgabe sämtlicher Symphonien. In twelve volumes, edited by H. C. Robbins Landon, Vienna, 1968.
At present this is the only complete edition of the Haydn symphonies. It is published in two formats: miniature scores (Universal Edition) and full scores (Doblinger).

Joseph Haydn, Sinfonien, herausgegeben vom Joseph Haydn-Institut, Köln, unter der Leitung von G. Feder, Munich, 1963– .
By 1973, about three dozen symphonies had been published.

HAYDN'S LIFE, WORK, LETTERS
IN ENGLISH

Adler, Guido, "Haydn and the Viennese Classical School," in *The Musical Quarterly,* XVIII (1932), 191–207.

Geiringer, Karl, *Haydn, a Creative Life in Music,* 2nd ed., reprinted with revisions, Berkeley and Los Angeles, 1968.

Gotwals, Vernon, *Joseph Haydn: Eighteenth-Century Gentleman and Genius,* Madison, Wisc., 1963.

Hadden, James Cuthbert, *Haydn,* revised ed., London, 1934.

Hughes, Rosemary, *Haydn,* London, 1950.

Landon, H. C. Robbins, *The Symphonies of Joseph Haydn,* London, 1955.

———— *Essays on the Viennese Classical Style,* New York, 1970.

———— (comp. and tr.) *The Collected Correspondence and London Notebooks of Joseph Haydn,* London, 1959.

Rosen, Charles, *The Classical Style,* New York, 1972.

Scott, Marion M., "Haydn in England," in *The Musical Quarterly,* XVIII (1932), 260–274.

Somfai, László, *Joseph Haydn: His Life in Contemporary Pictures,* New York, 1969.

HAYDN'S LIFE, WORK, LETTERS
IN GERMAN

Hoboken, Anthony van, *Joseph Haydn: thematisch-bibliographisches Werk-verzeichnis,* vol. I, Mainz, 1957; vol. II, 1971.

Larsen, Jens Peter, *Die Haydn-Überlieferung,* Copenhagen, 1939.

Pohl, Karl Ferdinand, *Mozart und Haydn in London,* Vienna, 1867.

———— *Joseph Haydn,* Leipzig, 1875, 1882. Completed by Hugo Botstiber, Leipzig, 1927.

Schmid, Ernst Fritz, *Joseph Haydn: ein Buch von Vorfahren und Heimat des Meisters,* Kassel, 1934.

KARL GEIRINGER (b. 1899) was curator of the library of the Gesellschaft der Musikfreunde in Vienna, from which position—traditionally connected with Haydn research—he wrote his first Haydn book, in the German language. Since moving to America, he has also worked in other areas (musical instruments, Brahms, Bach, the Bach family) but always returned to his original field of interest, editing a volume of Haydn's Scottish folksong arrangements and the hitherto unpublished opera *Orlando Paladino* for the collected edition of the composer's works. He was Professor of Music and Chairman of the Department of Graduate Studies in Music at Boston University, and served subsequently in the same capacity at the University of California, Santa Barbara.